The Last Place on Earth

John Wesley Claxton

───────────────────────────────

The Last Place on Earth

Vanguard Press

VANGUARD PAPERBACK

© Copyright 2024
John Wesley Claxton
Cover photograph Kurt Fries

The right of John Wesley Claxton to be identified as author of this work has been asserted by him in accordance with the Copyright, Designs and Patents Act 1988.

All Rights Reserved

No reproduction, copy or transmission of this publication may be made without written permission.
No paragraph of this publication may be reproduced, copied or transmitted save with the written permission of the publisher, or in accordance with the provisions of the Copyright Act 1956 (as amended).

Any person who commits any unauthorised act in relation to this publication may be liable to criminal prosecution and civil claims for damages.

A CIP catalogue record for this title is available from the British Library.

ISBN 978 1 80016 770 4

*Vanguard Press is an imprint of
Pegasus Elliot Mackenzie Publishers Ltd.*
www.pegasuspublishers.com

First Published in 2024

**Vanguard Press
Sheraton House Castle Park
Cambridge England**

Printed & Bound in Great Britain

For my father.

For time is the longest distance between two places.

- Tennessee Williams

NIGHT OF SEVEN DEER

They enter
stage left. In that moment

everything changes, the way a sudden snowfall
paints a new scene over the old yard.
Our hearts go out to them

as though they were our children.
They know so much more than we do.

They walk with great care
out of the woods. Someone must be sleeping there tonight
and they've promised to bring them news

of what the moon calls to their attention.

THE UNRAVELING

There was a smell like kerosene. And the sound,
sputtering and stammering,

of propeller-driven planes. Lumbering hulks
found their way out of the darkness

to their numbered gates. I loved and feared
the clamor, sitting high on my father's shoulders —

something important.
My uncle was coming home. I remember

the feeling of that. The gravity of the stories
he told. The weight of his hand on my head

as he measured my growth. The red silk
pillow he brought for my mother. And the look

in his eyes, as if he had forgotten something.
He had been gone and now he was home.

His uniform hanging in the hallway closet.

THE WOODLOT

It was ours though there was no fence around it.
Those couple of acres behind my aunt's house

in northern Indiana. We caught bluegill there,
claimed its hills for sledding, its trees for climbing

and more than once we saw a deer.
When we thought to do it, we picked handfuls

of lilies of the valley for our mothers who arranged
them in mason jars and put them on the windowsill.

We grew up, outgrew it. We disappeared
into steel mills in Gary or office buildings

in Chicago or one-story houses in nameless places.
We see each other again when one of us passes on.

The one who knew how to bait a hook. Then the one
who broke a collar bone flying from our tree house.

We stand there together, those of us left,
quiet as a stand of birch.

LIFE'S WORK

I start the day in the highest branches of the tree. It's something
    I learned from the birds, who have always held the advantage

        of perspective. I readily admit, each day I try to keep my head in the clouds
        for as long as I can.

    When I was younger
    I could fly: See life a mile away and find my way to it.

    Now I sit patiently and wait for things to come to me.
    Don't mistake that for sadness.

    I have things here on the ground.
    The delicate face of the purple orchid. The Dylan Thomas

        with the coffee-stained jacket. And the dog, still here.
        He's asleep at my feet.

HOLD ON

It's just like words to cut

both ways. To say one thing
and mean another.

Hold on, we say

to babies
and their first steps.

Wait, hold on, we say

when we meet
with the preposterous.

Hold on, we pray

at the sickbed
of a loved one.

Hold on, I say

to the baying of my friend. Hold on
to my gray shadow.

THIRD AND GUADALUPE

He was playing one chord, over
and over. Nothing pretty, but it was something

to lean on. He played
with persistence and restraint, the lone chord

a thin echo of the man. The old bones of his guitar
still made a good home for his hands.

But when he began to sing, the world opened
like a rose. It was a chant, maybe ancient,

that he sang in another tongue. His voice was high
and pleasing but full of sorrow. His song

a lamentation, maybe an elegy for beauty.
Itself a thing of beauty. It was enough

to still the busy street for just one moment. Just enough
to keep the two red-tailed hawks

circling in the sky.

1945

She chose her words carefully. Each,
a lily she placed on the page as if

testing ice. She wrote about her day.
Meeting friends at the local grocery,

falling in love with my father. In her hand,
in ink the color of night sky, a bird

skipped across the surface of the page, barely
touching it.

HARTSFIELD ASSISTED LIVING

Bob still drives. His pristine two-tone Plymouth
is the envy of all the men. He threatens to take

some of the women out for a spin and they laugh
and call him a rogue. Their lives there, together,

are gently lived. Bob tells me stories. And you can
see the memories alive in his eyes. Life still

stubbornly there, waiting for nothing. Maybe
we owe this much to each other. Our stories

told well. An arm around a shoulder. Time,
a Stardust Yellow Plymouth, cruises in the distance.

AN ACT OF KINDNESS

We gather around the foot of her bed
while my aunt sings *Take Me Out to the Ballgame*.

She sings, not like someone afraid they might
miss a note, but the way it must be sung

at the ballpark: loud and without apology.
We have no choice. We sing along —

and after the first or second time, we sing
with conviction. No one cares if they never

get back. There is nothing else
to do. We all sing

and in singing we remember. A feeling.
Bright lights against the darkness. Dogs chasing

barking in delight. Laughter
cartwheeling down a hill.

LOOKING BACK

We all watched, letting the dinner cool on our plates,
    as my grandson climbed the stairs for the first time.

With his mom right behind him, he convinced
his arms and legs that it was the right thing to do.

We shouted the usual words of encouragement,
but I don't think he needed them.

He was resolute. Listening to something
the rest of us could not hear. And as he neared

the top, he turned and looked at us, a space explorer
drifting through the galaxy, looking back at Earth.

HOMELESS

If I have forgotten anything, it is how to be humble
in the presence of beauty. The old school ways

of being able to learn something from anything.
A demonstration of time passing, for example;

as found in granite or the speed of light explained
in the shape of a butterfly wing. I want to be in awe

today. See a little something that brings me to my
knees.
A little razzle dazzle at sunrise. Or just a song

from a lone turtle dove. Something to remind me
of bounty or goodness or justice. Something to remind
me

that there are no strangers here. That we all
come from the same mother.

BLOOMINGTON, MINNESOTA

They fly in perfect formation. Canada Geese so close
   to the ground, I can hear the sound of their wings.

   It's a whispering cadence that hints of an early spring,
   a sound
   so beautiful it makes the silence that follows
   profound.

   It's a silence I heard once in a cathedral in Florence.
   Both an absence and a presence. Something with me,

   something within me. The silence of all the things I
   do
   not know or understand. Deep. Burgundy. Dark

   as the quiet at the end of conversation. The silence
   that surrounds us all today. As if some of us were
   waiting,

   just you and I, for one of us to speak.

THE GARDEN

In a small town of simple houses, my grandparents
    lived less than a mile from us. Their house was the
    oldest.

    It smelled of good things baking and a cellar
    full of miracles—my sister and I once watched a stray
    cat

    birth her litter in that darkness. In the front yard
    was an ancient oak where mourning doves nested—

    the back was split by a cinder path that led
    to the tool shed, one half gone to weed

    the other half tilled every spring.
    That was where my grandfather taught me,

    with much patience and silence, how to give tomatoes
    a start,
    where to put the green beans, how deep to plant a row
    of

    sweet corn seeds. He showed me how to use a walk
    behind tiller
    and how much watering was enough. I remember
    everything

though he never, the whole time, said more
than five words. And in early summer, in the weeds,

I'd get down on my hands and knees between the
plants.
Standing above me, my grandmother waved her dish
towel

at mosquitoes while she sang her hymns. A single row
of sweetest corn; when the silk turned brown, it was
ready to be harvested.

THE MYSTERY OF DISTANCE

Early in the day we saw an ox hit by a truck.
The blunt sound of the impact took more

than the ox's life. We were glad
to have our work. It was something familiar.

We were traveling to Bamako in Mali
to meet with farmers in a nearby village.

They told us of our good fortune. We had missed
the great famine that had taken so many. The drought

had left the land sallow and indifferent. Their stories
were their gift to us. We offered ours in return.

What we learned was honest as land without water.
Near the end of the day the clouds came, and then—

rain. An unforgiving torrent.
We ran from it,

or because of it, like we did when we were children.
Some falling. Some laughing. Some standing

in surrender: that was the sound, arms outstretched,
of the truck hitting the ox. We made it

to our tent, little more than a roof of tattered canvas
while the villagers huddled

in a lean-to a few yards across the way. We looked
at each other across the distance. The gray rain

came down in centuries.

MOTORCADE, DETROIT 1971

The line begins at the old Lutheran church
and goes on for blocks, snaking its way past

Mahler's Service Station and, half a mile further,
past Dettmering's Tavern where a few customers

have come to the window to pay their respects.
Lights on in the middle of the day, not for seeing

but to be seen, the motorcade idles in silence,
a few drivers fussing with their rearview mirrors

for a better look at the drivers behind them. Each one leads
and follows; they seem to know when to inch

forward, the lumbering
Detroit cars pushing slowly through the town

to the cemetery. A policeman on his motorcycle
waiting at the gate.

MILWAUKEE NORTH

I overhear the passenger in front of me
talking about the glory days of this train,

the days when there was a bar car crowded and
loud, people drinking, unknotting the workday,

traveling from one world to another,
the men wearing suits

and wide ties, smelling of newsprint and
martinis, the women rakish or demure

wearing hats to match. *Those were the days*
muses the passenger in front of me,

his voice bittersweet with longing. I settle
for the view out the window. The conductor

narrates in monotone: Mayfair. Forest Glen.
Edgebrook. The coffee shops and restaurants.

Deerfield. Lake Forest. Libertyville. The conductor
waits
for each passenger to step off the train. His uniform

is still neatly pressed at the end of the day. White shirt.

Dark blue jacket and tie. He looks south, then north:

The empty tracks shimmer in the afternoon sun.

HINDSIGHT

It's a sandbox. Built by hand by my dad
who placed it for shade near a tree.

He painted it bright red and cut, carefully,
the sweet-smelling pine boards that he nailed

into the corners, four places for me to sit
and play. And I would play there for hours,

making sand roads and mountains and rivers
of sand, though at that time I didn't know yet

the story of that sand, how each grain
had lived as a stone of quartz the size of a
pomegranate

and had traveled on the wind miles and miles
for millions of years—and then miles and miles back.

The wind and the miles and the sun
and the rain had made each grain a perfect sphere,

a whole small world I'd balance on the tip of my
finger—
the only audience, my dog Dizzy, who looked on.

THE GOOD CHINA

We found it in a box in her closet.
Never opened. Never used. Each plate

kept from the next by a measured
square of cardboard, which fit neatly

into the bottom of the plate
above it, and so on. The good china

stood always at the ready in case of an
occasion. The fact that

the box was never opened is the bitter
poetry, I suppose. All those unused years she spent

tending to the needs of others. Her cousin.
Her mother. The people at work.

So many of them. One upon the other. And
so on, and so on.

SILENT MOVIE

The clouds came early today, so we heard it
before we saw it, the red biplane.

Our eyes scanned the sky for proof: Two red wings, a sudden
flash of sunlight. Sight and

sound not quite in sync, but
pleasing, playing like a silent movie, the orchestra off

a beat, the picture
catching up, the whole thing a brilliant show:

A gentle loop. A leveling off. And—
gone. Some years earlier

I watched a lone white swan as it swam

against the current on the St. Joe River.
I watched it for a long time

trying to understand if it was leading the way
or left behind.

The clouds came early that day, too.
Balanced delicately on the surface of the water.

IN CONSIDERATION OF THE CLOUDS

If you are in a pond, it's best to walk
gently, waist deep, trying not
to disturb the white clouds.

In the pond, if you take small steps,
you might count the ripples—
or watch the progress of angels—
depending on your mood

—and the mood of the pond, where it's best
to tread lightly if you want to feel
the weightlessness of the beautiful shapes
best seen from a distance falling gently

over the pond in which you are standing
waist-deep, trying not to disturb the clouds.

TANGO

Any day that begins with pancakes
is a good day. I offer nothing

more profound than that.
Think of us as children

coming down the stairs for breakfast.
We eat whatever is put before us.

We are here.
It is good.

And there is no question
that cannot be

answered by love. I believe
or maybe I once did

that if you could live your whole life
in a single day, there could be nothing

more perfect. A kind of daylong moment
of clarity. Earth, moon and sun

coming into focus as one. Forest
and sea and all the animals

living and breathing
the same moment with us, wonder

upon wonder, you and I
dancing the tango Milonguero style. Close,

until the end.

SHELTER

My uncle had a cinder block basement, bleak
and unfinished, but with a cook stove

and long wooden tables, big enough for forty-one
cousins—and their mothers and fathers—to sit at

and eat. At least once a year we would gather there
in the dim light of bare bulbs and be family, the
cousins

tumbling over each other like a litter of puppies,
the aunts and uncles spooling up

the silent film of their shared childhood, and—lush
in the air—the smell of pot roast and steamed
vegetables.

I know now that we remember ourselves in each
other. Uncle Roy the stoic. Aunt Doris wrapped in joy,

the generosity of Lillian. It's there in the photographs.
You can see it in our eyes.

Plain as concrete.

PRIMER

Maybe life isn't so profound after all,
a thought that comes to mind

while I'm waiting for the train.
If you could find a way to strip away

all the weight of metaphor, maybe then
you would have the beginning

of something very good.
Say, if you were able to get down

on your hands and knees,
not in a religious kind of way,

but in an effort to make yourself small,
maybe small

as an atom. In an attempt to feel
the forces at work, understand how

it all comes together, predict
your own behavior. Maybe today

is the day I see it all.
Maybe a beauty so simple and austere

it'll make me weep.
The train arrives, the train leaves;

I can see myself growing smaller,
kneeling beside the track.

DRIVING TO SWAKOPMUND

They have a geography we cannot memorize.
Mapless shapes, the dunes stir in their sleep.

I want to lie down with them and let the wind
sculpt me into a sleek cheetah, a wave

in search of an ocean. When I have become another
and still another

shifting shape, these stars won't be the stars
I will know, nor this sky. And that voice I hear

carried by the wind on grains of sand,
that is not your voice.

GLACIOLOGY

The bit
of question
left on your face, the way it brightens
your eyes: Just so.

I suppose an ice age is out of the question.
I was hoping to keep things just as they are.

Even the way you're looking at me now –
This is this, and this
is all.

Even the thought
you're having. That you can't
keep from having – about what's next.

Whatever it is, it's perfect, crystalline in form.

HYMN OF THE UNIVERSE

Though the notes are plainly printed
on the page, each of us listens differently.

For some, it's a surprisingly sad song.
You might think with the stars and all,

the brilliance of the Milky Way and such,
it would be a cheery tune. Trumpets

making a statement. A flourish of French horns.
Cascading piano solo. But only the string section

shows up tonight. Long bowed tones
that call to us like mourning doves and whisper

rumors of a galaxy none of us will ever see.
Hope, sings the cello in riposte, knowing full well

the fate of all the stars.

INDIGO

I can see the whole storm from here. Dark
curtain of indigo, the rain claiming a spot

miles away in the flatlands. I can see it all
from this distance, beginning

to end, but hear nothing. Feel nothing.
It's someone else's rain today,

someone else's parade or picnic, plan
for a perfect day.

Someone else is gathering
his children as first drops begin to fall.

He might be anxious. A father
like me, maybe. Worrying much over what little

he can do. This
is that. Someone else's rain.

Somewhere in the flatlands. Someone
else's worry. Someone else's joy, or any

other feeling. Someone else's friendless sentence
citing age

and cause of death.

Dark curtain. A flash: then bouts of thunder. Between them, I'm
counting the seconds.

STRAY

The dog sits shivering in the cold.
Ears back flat against his head.

He's been rescued by a stranger, who has brought
a bowl of water and news of the owner

on his way. With the sound

of my approach, he turns and looks at me, eyes
filled with hope and fear. He hopes there is something

about me that is familiar. He has a story to tell.
Don't we all. And he just wants

someone to listen. The sound of my voice.
The feel of my hand. The scent of a certain kind

of fear.

THE HANGING GARDENS OF BABYLON

It's nice to hear the sound of the gulls
this morning, returning

to our frozen lake. With no chance of fish
today, they are simply here for play.

They ride the winter wind in great looping circles,
round and round, white wings

drifting through the blue sky. I watch until they fly
away. Then watch the empty sky.

WEIGHTS AND MEASURES

It's something we can all agree on. The untarnished truth
of a gram or an ounce. The reliability

of dense metals and gravity. The actuality
of the elements. These are the things

that hold us to the Earth. The weight of conscience.
A measure of humility. Beneath our feet, ancient

gears and pulleys turn us toward the sun of another
day.
There, in a time as certain as the next centimeter

we will continue to consider the meaning of life, of a
life
well lived. Weights and measures in balance.

Loved ones loved. Birth holding its own against death.
And then,
the sun moves. The shadows change.

The scale is tipped.

MORNING LIGHT

While traveling at the same speed
as other light, morning light reaches first

the hopeful. Those who've misspent yesterday's
promise
of something luminous—clean white sheets

on a clothesline still waiting for the breeze
that never came.

We are the ones looking up
this morning, heads held high, searching

the hilltops and the treetops. Hoping
for the first sign of gold on green. A sign

that the laws of physics will hold true this day
like every day, which may lead to other truths as well.

UNDERSTANDING

I sometimes think if I could understand
one thing, I would understand everything.

The way a rose unfolds, for example.
Take the tiniest detail. One petal. Knowing

when to curl. Just that.

TIME. AND TIME AGAIN

The pocket watch that traveled from Germany
with my grandfather after the war now keeps time

with my cousin in Munster, Indiana. There's a hat,
once stylish, that my sister-in-law dares to wear

on occasion. And on the dressing table of my aunt,
a comb and brush still cling to each other

after all these years, not quite at home. It seems time
finds a place for things we once kept in the attic.

A Bolo tie with bravado, doilies, neatly stacked.
The sediment of our lives gets another life before
turning.

THE ELOQUENCE OF BONES

There is nothing frightening about them.
Two skeletons, a man and a woman,

captured in a moment of casual conversation.
Or, so it seems. The photograph, unexpectedly

beautiful, is one of hundreds in this book
of skeletons. Human and animal, we're all

here. From the European hedgehog—every bone
its nose, sniffing out food—to the black-crowned

night heron, regal even without its plumage.
Here is the cane toad, about to leap. The sailfish,

knifing through the water. The wood mouse,
begging for forgiveness. Across millennia, so little

has changed. What is so, is so. The hunters
hunt—and are hunted. Fear, say the bones

of the mountain hare. While the panda holds out
his paw in good will: eloquent and silent.

SATURN

I'm looking at pictures of Saturn tonight
imagining a trip there later in the fall.

The rings alone inspire wonder—
some cosmic toy set spinning in space.

But the story of Saturn is the story
of its moons. Prometheus, Titan, Hyperion:

the names burning with passion: *Father
of Fire, Race of Gods. Heavenly Light.*

If Saturn is where you go to fall in love,
you can choose from the light of sixty-two

moons. Pan or Telesto. Daphnis. Calypso.
Each has a story four billion years old.

A man and a woman walk
into a bar. A chancing of hydrocarbons.

A dark tempest sidles up to a shimmering
aurora. A tilted axis of inuendo? Even at

a billion kilometers from Earth, you know
what happens next, and next – you know.

OAK

All this time, I've kept the photographs
hanging in the hallway. My mother

leaning against a giant oak, daring
the camera to come closer. My father

in a similar pose, smiling at the world.
Nothing is as simple as we remember.

The tree. The black Packard. The sound
of mourning doves. I've lived both

their lives over and over again, trying
to remember songs my father taught me,

trying to divine the farm girl shyness
of my mother. I'm searching

for a small truth. I could carry it with me.
A certain watchfulness.

ON BEING REMEMBERED

I've tried. With all my understanding
of the many ages and all my longing

for the most distant stars, to be
something more. Short

of sacred, unworthy
of herald, but something

more than dust. A head-nod
among my colleagues. A footnote

in a book. Simply one touch,
nothing much or more.

I have learned, and only just,
that the smallest living things

will be here long after we are gone.
There is nothing else I know.

NO ACCOUNTING

There is a wobble in the Earth's rotation
that puzzles scientists. Not to mention

the complexity of language, the rhythm
of the seasons, the migration of the arctic tern.

None of us understand love, the upbringing
of children or how to change, the oil filter

on a '64 Impala. All I can do is gaze at you now and marvel
at the genealogy of your hazel eyes.

FALLING

Having reached a certain age, I no longer do it
with grace. Just this morning I left my pride

lying on the icy sidewalk. First, an unexpected curtsy,
then a penguin trying to fly. While recovering

my footing, I remembered a time, long ago, when
falling
was part of a good time – an exclamation point, really,

on joy. And a bruised knee
or a nick on the chin was just a short timeout

between leaps and falls. But when you start walking
like an old man, you take things more seriously.

You learn that it's not the fall, it's the fear
that pulls you down. The Earth

is pulling me closer, whispering in my ear.

A GATHERING IS CALLED A PLAGUE

While we were sleeping they filled the trees,
shadowy leaves, a thousand great-tail grackle.

There is no murmuration here. No aerial ballet.
None of the artfulness of gathering starlings. The grackle

attack. They occupy. And their victory cry
is a screech, the forcing of a rusted hinge.

It serves a warning to the winged and wingless
alike. Their outrage rules the night

and draws a line—us
and them. They come in mid-August.

By April, they're gone. We live on our side
most of the year.

WHERE LOVE COMES FROM

There are words for it. *Iram. Kātal. Uruku.*
Crystalline breath of snowflake.

But it is older than words, words themselves
unnamed, continents

undiscovered. A river's ancestry
is infinite. So too is love's.

Mostly it is quiet.
A candle burns.

A thought, carried on the evening breeze,
turns the page of an open book.

You can sometimes see it in a photograph,
something cyphered in the grain.

BEFORE MONGOLIA

We spent the night in China.
The hotel, brightly lit and unfamiliar

was welcoming, but we could not sleep.
The next day we would stand in silence

before the mountains of the Gobi:
Qilian, *Altai* and *Helan*. We would hear

the story of the eagle hunter
and learn the wonder of his sky.

But that night, sleepless, restless and sleepless,
I opened the window to the night and listened.

In the distance, somewhere in the darkness,
the simple sound of boots on snow.

Each footfall sharp and pronounced,
crisp as the night air, well-formed.

I stood at the window and listened—
a lone man

came out of darkness passed through
a pool of light and disappeared

into darkness again. The sound
of his boots on the snow

calmed me. Towards morning,
I fell asleep listening to the mountains.

COME, RAIN

This is no night to be alone.
There is too much truth

in the rain. It's found a calling –
falling – in a rhythm that will not stop.

If you go into it, I'll go into it,
my body angled forward

so the greatest number of drops
can make themselves

be felt. That one
carried a message from my father.

This one, bittersweet, something a love
lost. For the friend I could have

helped: Rain. Rain
on my silence, my all-too-often. Rain.

Rain on rain, unstopping as my
father's need. His words to me

were a warning.
He could not heed himself.

THOUGHTS ON ORNITHOLOGY

Between first love and last breath,
there should be at least one conversation

that lasts all night
and arrives in the morning at a full-blown epiphany—

the sun coming up burning gold
sunlight illuminating the day

and the night, both. It should be breathtaking.
But maybe I ask

too much. It could be, maybe, just a moment—
lasting long enough to let our coffees cool—

When our eyes met, all of history
was there, an open book, and we read it together

for the first time. A moment not unlike
that of the ornithologist who,

having traveled to the island off the coast
of Indonesia for just this reason, hears the song

of an undiscovered bird.

HOW TO WRITE A POEM

First,
draw an imaginary line
from the tip of your finger
to a point in space
3,000 miles above the north pole
of Neptune,

to be precise.

Along the line
place every moment of your life.

Start with something simple.

The time you lost a mitten
in the snow.

Then something big.

Like the birth
of your daughter.

Continue to place every moment
along the line,
each one
next to the other,

until you have a long line of all the moments
reaching out from the tip of your finger
to the planet farthest from the sun.

Hold onto that line
and you have memory.

Let go
and you have the first line of a poem.

TWILIGHT

Tonight, a small bowl of Kalamata olives between us,
we've learned about the Gingko trees in China.

They live a thousand years or more.

ABOUT THE MOON

It is Galileo's. He was the first to see
its valleys bowing down to its mountains.

We parse the darkness from the light and see
the truth, ancient and waiting, the Earth

beneath our feet, this is our truth.
The tree with the singing bird

is our way forward. We stand here together
in the blue calm of the moon, understanding

light and dark. Each
a gift like the days themselves.

The singing bird never forgets its song.

ALL OUR FRIENDS CAME HERE TO DANCE

We were such starry-eyed children, arriving on the shores
of the planet. Hope tied in bundles, our faces

    shining: the mountains wept; we bowed with great
    respect. We held etiquette

    sacred, and held close the promise of our first dance.
    But at some point we said we didn't know

    it'd be like this. That happiness
    would have, tagging along, it's always-sad friend. The
    one

    sitting at the end of a row of empty chairs.
    Hands pressed together in his lap.

DANGEROUSLY CLOSE TO HAPPINESS

The morning *en pointe*, a delicate balance
of blue and white. Nothing demands

the attention of my next thought. Just the lake
stretching to reach the shore. Nothing perilous

or pending or on the verge of collapse.
Nothing said. Nothing done. Nothing feared.

Nothing of nothing. The day contains its own demands
and moves its own free will toward

the night. Here's something that feels
like a beginning. Something that moves

with silence and grace. The morning, *en pointe*,
a balance of blue and white.

CROSSING THE RIVER

We slept in, a Christmas Eve tradition;
once awake, we set about finding familiar things

in the day. I built a fire and found Sinatra
on the radio. The kids made sugar cookies

like they had seen their mother do. It was all
like it had always been, and we were together.

When my son called us to the window,
I hoped it was snowing. But there, like statues

placed at the river's edge, were two deer.
A doe and a buck. Heads held high, their backs

to us. Standing together, they looked across
to the far side, and at a moment

they seemed to understand together, they leapt
into the water and swam easily across.

We stood watching from the windows.

LOCK TALONS, FREE FALL

They pull at the horizon. Two magnificent
eagles, their talons locked in a death spiral.

There is a certain kind of romance in falling.
We remember it: the sky-spinning ground-rushing

beauty of things coming into view
too fast to understand them, points of reference

no longer relevant, the tree is the sky is the tree.
Having fallen once, we fear and desire falling

again, and from greater heights. Eagles do it
right in a mate-for-life ritual several thousand

feet in the air. From that height, words are small.
Maybe we'll get it right this time, we think to ourselves,

as the earth comes spinning into view.

NIGHT SCHOOL

They fly in a line, the seagulls of the Côte d'Azur.
    I watch it, the line, and I wonder for a moment

        if each bird's position is earned by level of skill.
        For those at the rear, there is, perhaps, a certain tip

        of the wing yet to be mastered. A sense of grace
        or poise that might come with age and follows years

        of practice, of asking, wh*y fly at all?* A question left
        unanswered by the night sky and the rising moon.

SLEEP FAST

When we visited our grandmother, my sister and I
    would stay up late watching movies

    on the old black and white Philco,
    the sound turned down so low

    it was nothing more than a murmur of us
    telling stories, stories so increasingly outrageous

    that we'd laugh loud enough
    to wake my grandmother, who'd appear in the door

    Sleep fast, she'd command, pretending to be mad,
    the stoic image of John Wayne

    flickering on the wall just behind her.

THE LIGHT

The white heron passing over the lake just there
is one place to start: The smallest thing can illuminate

almost everything. I caress the spine of a book:
the glacier I stood on once, glistening like history,

shines white. I spin the globe and with my finger
stop it. Right there I found a certain way to see the
stars.

THIS DAY

Leaves me breathless. This moment.
Beyond the ordinary needs of my body.

From here, I look out
on the days remaining, dog-eared

pages in the story of my life. Their promise.
Their passing. Shapes and forms.

Melodies of song I may never know
the words to. I want to be god,

the god of the world, all that I can see,
all that I can touch. But I am only

a man, meant to bow
in sacred places. Suitable for burial.

A GOOD LIFE

Start with the physics of it and you will find it
less difficult to measure. Calculate its weight

and mass, the speed with which it moves through
the universe. All of this governed by the law

of gravity and the passing of time. Once
you have the math of it, the rest is like a word

in one language that cannot be translated
into another. *Jijivisha*. Hindi for an English

approximation, one word we might say describes
an intense desire to live life to the fullest.

But again, no translation.
Take today. A moment in passing. I looked out

across the frozen lake. Brilliant sun blinding
the ice. On it I saw two skaters. Their dark silhouettes.

They were skating and they were dancing.
Momentum sent them apart—and their eyes, it
seemed,

the pull of them, drew their bodies back together.

Even from this distance

I could see their love. *Koi No Yokan.* Eyes burning like suns.

THE LAST PLACE ON EARTH

It would make leaving so much more like arriving
if I could choose my last place on Earth.

It would be more like planning a trip to Florence
with my wife and being mindful of the tourist traffic

at the Piazza Duomo in early fall. What a gift!
To be able to pick the time and more importantly

the place. One of those cellar bars in Prague
comes to mind. Me, sitting among a small group

of friends, my hands wrapped around a cold stein
of Pilsner Urquell as we tell the stories we all know

the ends of. Or maybe those shifting sand dunes
along the Namibian coast where an afternoon hike

ends at the outset. Or maybe I'd rather somewhere
closer. A page in a book I've been meaning to read.

Me, a mark between pages of things
I've yet to learn. I would read out loud

the way you sometimes like me to, every word
a star. Brilliant, then dimming.

ACKNOWLEDGEMENTS

Grateful acknowledgment is made to the editors of the following publications, in which these poems, sometimes in earlier versions, appeared.

Atticus Review: *Homeless*
Beyond Words Literary Magazine: *The Last Place On Earth*
East by Northeast: *Looking Back*
Poetry East: *The Last Place On Earth*
Poets Choice: *An Act of Kindness*

ABOUT THE AUTHOR

John Claxton grew up in a small town in northern Illinois. After graduating from Butler University, he moved to Chicago and began a long career in advertising. Midway through this career, he worked on a project with Billy Collins. He decided, then and there, to become a poet and has never looked back. He has had poems published in the *Atticus Review, Beyond Words, East by Northeast, Poetry East and Poets Choice*. This is his first book of poems.

www.ingramcontent.com/pod-product-compliance
Lightning Source LLC
Chambersburg PA
CBHW060622080526
44585CB00013B/939